THE SUPREME

ROGER FEDERER

TRIVIA AND QUIZ BOOK

BY: JACKSON WELLS

Table of Contents

INTRODUCTION TO ROGER FEDERER

Roger Federer, widely regarded as one of the greatest tennis players in history, has amassed a remarkable array of achievements throughout his illustrious career. Holding the record for the most Grand Slam titles won by a male player, Federer's incredible prowess on the court has earned him a total of 20 major singles championships. His versatility is evident in his success on different surfaces, capturing titles at Wimbledon a record eight times, the Australian Open six times, the US Open five times, and the French Open once. Federer's enduring dominance has extended to the prestigious ATP Tour Finals, where he secured the title six times. With a record-breaking 310 weeks spent as the World No. 1, Federer's consistency and longevity at the top of the rankings showcase his unparalleled skill and resilience. Beyond the statistics, Federer's artistry, sportsmanship, and unwavering dedication to the sport have solidified his legacy as a tennis icon and a global ambassador for the game.

HOBBIES AND INTEREST
QUESTION TIME!

1. What is Roger Federer's favorite hobby outside of tennis?

    a) Golf

    b) Cooking

    c) Skiing

    d) Reading

2. Federer is known to have a special interest in which other sport?

    a) Soccer

    b) Basketball

    c) Golf

    d) Swimming

3. Which musical instrument does Federer play?

    a) Piano

    b) Violin

    c) Guitar

    d) Drums

4. Federer has expressed a love for which type of cuisine?

　a) Italian

　b) Japanese

　c) Swiss

　d) Mexican

5. In interviews, Federer has mentioned his enjoyment of which outdoor activity?

　a) Hiking

　b) Fishing

　c) Cycling

　d) Gardening

6. What book genre does Roger Federer often mention as his favorite?

　a) Mystery/Thriller

　b) Science Fiction

　c) Biography

　d) Historical Fiction

7. Federer is known to be a fan of which movie genre?

a) Action

b) Comedy

c) Drama

d) Science Fiction

8. Which language, other than his native Swiss German, is Federer known to speak fluently?

a) French

b) Spanish

c) Italian

d) English

9. Federer has been spotted attending which major sporting event as a spectator?

a) Super Bowl

b) FIFA World Cup

c) Olympics

d) Wimbledon

10. What is Federer's stance on social media?

a) Active user

b) Rarely uses it

c) Doesn't use social media

d) Has a social media manager

11. Federer has a collection of watches. Which luxury watch brand is he associated with?

a) Rolex

b) Omega

c) Patek Philippe

d) Audemars Piguet

12. What is Federer's preferred vacation destination?

a) Maldives

b) Swiss Alps

c) Caribbean

d) French Riviera

13. In interviews, Federer has expressed an interest in which form of art?

a) Painting

b) Sculpture

c) Photography

d) Literature

14. Federer's favorite type of music is often described as:

a) Classical

b) Rock

c) Pop

d) Jazz

15. Which charitable cause is Federer actively involved in?

a) Education

b) Environmental Conservation

c) Healthcare

d) All of the above

16. What is Federer's favorite type of workout?

a) Yoga

b) Weightlifting

c) Cardio

d) Pilates

17. Federer has been involved in the design of his own line of:

a) Clothing

b) Shoes

c) Tennis Rackets

d) Sunglasses

18. Which tennis tournament is Federer known to attend as a spectator when not playing?

a) French Open

b) Australian Open

c) US Open

d) Wimbledon

19. Federer has expressed admiration for which historical figure?

a) Albert Einstein

b) Leonardo da Vinci

c) Mahatma Gandhi

d) Winston Churchill

20. What is Federer's favorite type of cuisine to cook at home?

a) Pasta

b) Barbecue

c) Sushi

d) Desserts

21. Federer has mentioned enjoying which type of board game?

a) Chess

b) Monopoly

c) Scrabble

d) Risk

22. Which type of movie does Federer enjoy watching during his downtime?

a) Romantic Comedy

b) Action-Thriller

c) Documentary

d) Animated

23. Federer's interest in which Olympic sport is well-known?

a) Swimming

b) Gymnastics

c) Tennis

d) Archery

24. In interviews, Federer has mentioned his appreciation for:

a) Vintage Cars

b) Modern Art

c) Technology Gadgets

d) Antique Furniture

25. What type of cuisine did Federer explore during his travels that left a lasting impression on him?

a) Indian

b) Chinese

c) Thai

d) Mexican

26. Federer has collaborated with a famous sports brand for a line of:

a) Tennis Apparel

b) Running Shoes

c) Golf Equipment

d) Swimwear

27. Which wildlife conservation cause has Federer supported?

a) Elephant Conservation

b) Marine Conservation

c) Tiger Conservation

d) Polar Bear Conservation

28. Federer has been involved in the promotion of which environmental initiative?

a) Renewable Energy

b) Clean Water Access

c) Plastic Waste Reduction

d) Reforestation

29. Federer has expressed an interest in which form of technology?

a) Virtual Reality

b) Artificial Intelligence

c) Space Exploration

d) Sustainable Technology

30. In interviews, Federer has shared his enjoyment of:

a) Wine Tasting

b) Coffee Brewing

c) Tea Ceremony

d) Cocktail Mixing

ANSWERS

1. b) Cooking

2. a) Soccer

3. a) Piano

4. c) Swiss

5. b) Fishing

6. c) Biography

7. a) Action

8. a) French

9. c) Olympics

10. b) Rarely uses it

11. a) Rolex

12. b) Swiss Alps

13. c) Photography

14. a) Classical

15. d) All of the above

16. a) Yoga

17. c) Tennis Rackets

18. d) Wimbledon

19. b) Leonardo da Vinci

20. b) Barbecue

21. c) Scrabble

22. c) Documentary

23. c) Tennis

24. a) Vintage Cars

25. c) Thai

26. a) Tennis Apparel

27. c) Tiger Conservation

28. c) Plastic Waste Reduction

29. b) Artificial Intelligence

30. a) Wine Tasting

FAN EXPERIENCES AND EVENTS
QUESTION TIME!

1. Which Grand Slam tournament is known for its iconic "Fan Week" that Federer actively participates in?

a) Australian Open

b) French Open

c) Wimbledon

d) US Open

2. Federer is known for organizing an exhibition event called:

a) Roger's Rally

b) Federer's Fiesta

c) The Fed Express

d) Match for Africa

3. In which year did Federer play the first "Match for Africa" exhibition?

a) 2008

b) 2010

c) 2014

d) 2018

4. What is the primary purpose of the "Match for Africa" events?

a) Showcasing new talents

b) Raising funds for charitable causes

c) Celebrating Grand Slam victories

d) Promoting tennis in underprivileged areas

5. Federer has hosted exhibition matches in unique locations, including:

a) Mount Everest

b) Burj Khalifa

c) Machu Picchu

d) The Great Wall of China

6. In 2020, Federer organized an event called "The Match in Africa." Who was his opponent?

a) Rafael Nadal

b) Novak Djokovic

c) Andy Murray

d) Serena Williams

7. Which global city hosted the "The Match in Africa 6" event in 2020?

a) Cape Town

b) New York

c) London

d) Sydney

8. Federer often interacts with fans through which social media platform?

a) Instagram

b) Twitter

c) Facebook

d) TikTok

9. What is the name of the official fan club for Roger Federer?

a) Federer's Fanatics

b) Roger's Raiders

c) The FedFans

d) Federer's Faithful

10. Federer's fanbase is collectively referred to as:

a) RF Nation

b) Fed Family

c) Roger's Realm

d) The Federer Flock

11. In 2019, Federer participated in a charity event named:

a) Match for Unity

b) Rally for Relief

c) Aces for Change

d) Points for Purpose

12. How does Federer often express gratitude to his fans during tournaments?

a) Personalized autographs

b) Social media shoutouts

c) Fan meet-and-greets

d) On-court interviews

13. Federer has been known to surprise fans by:

a) Handing out merchandise

b) Joining them in the stands

c) Organizing impromptu matches

d) All of the above

14. What is the name of the initiative where fans can submit questions for Federer to answer during tournaments?

a) Ask Roger

b) Roger's Q&A

c) Federer's Forum

d) Fans Ask Fed

15. Federer's autograph is often stylized with:

a) A smiley face

b) His initials "RF"

c) A tennis ball sketch

d) A crown symbol

16. In which year did Federer launch his official emoji on Twitter?

a) 2015

b) 2017

c) 2019

d) 2021

17. What is the name of the event where Federer plays against celebrities and fellow tennis players for charity?

a) Serve for Good

b) Set for a Cause

c) Aces for Charity

d) Smash for Hope

18. Fans can purchase official Federer merchandise at:

a) Grand Slam tournaments

b) Online store

c) Exclusive fan events

d) All of the above

19. Federer has a tradition of tossing his used tennis towels to fans. Which tournament is famous for this ritual?

a) Wimbledon

b) Australian Open

c) Roland Garros

d) US Open

20. What is the name of the fan-created initiative where fans wave red and white cards during Federer's matches?

a) Roger's Wave

b) FedFans' Fiesta

c) Swiss Support

d) RF Rally

21. In 2007, Federer played an exhibition match on a specially-built court on:

a) Lake Geneva

b) Sydney Harbour

c) Central Park

d) The Eiffel Tower

22. Federer has expressed interest in creating a fan experience similar to:

a) Comic-Con

b) Music Festivals

c) TED Talks

d) Food and Wine Expos

23. Federer has collaborated with a sports brand to create limited-edition fan merchandise. Which brand is it?

a) Nike

b) Adidas

c) Uniqlo

d) Puma

24. Fans often bring banners and signs with which popular phrase to Federer's matches?

a) "Federer Forever"

b) "RF Rules"

c) "Roger That"

d) "GOAT"

25. Federer has been known to send personal messages and gifts to:

   a) Random fans on social media

   b) Long-time supporters

   c) Fans attending specific tournaments

   d) All of the above

26. What is the name of the annual fan vote organized by the ATP that Federer often wins?

   a) Player of the Year

   b) Fan Favorite Award

   c) Sportsmanship Award

   d) Comeback Player of the Year

27. Federer's interaction with young fans often involves:

   a) Tennis clinics

   b) Storytime sessions

   c) Handing out signed tennis balls

   d) All of the above

28. Federer's official website features a dedicated section for:

a) Fan Art

b) Fan Stories

c) Fan Club Membership

d) Fan Polls

29. What is the name of the annual fan-led initiative to celebrate Federer's birthday on social media?

a) Roger's Day

b) Federer Fest

c) #RFBirthday

d) Roger's Celebration

30. Federer has expressed interest in creating a fan experience that involves:

a) Virtual Reality Tours

b) Live Q&A Sessions

c) Fan Meet-and-Greets

d) All of the above

ANSWERS

1. c) Wimbledon

2. d) Match for Africa

3. c) 2014

4. b) Raising funds for charitable causes

5. c) Machu Picchu

6. a) Rafael Nadal

7. a) Cape Town

8. b) Twitter

9. c) The FedFans

10. a) RF Nation

11. b) Rally for Relief

12. b) Social media shoutouts

13. d) All of the above

14. a) Ask Roger

15. c) A tennis ball sketch

16. b) 2017

17. b) Set for a Cause

18. d) All of the above

19. d) US Open

20. d) RF Rally

21. c) Central Park

22. c) TED Talks

23. a) Nike

24. d) "GOAT"

25. d) All of the above

26. b) Fan Favorite Award

27. d) All of the above

28. a) Fan Art

29. c) #RFBirthday

30. d) All of the above

CAREER ACHIEVEMENTS

QUESTION TIME!

1. How many Grand Slam singles titles has Roger Federer won as of 2022?

    a) 18

    b) 20

    c) 22

    d) 24

2. Federer holds the record for the most Wimbledon singles titles. How many Wimbledon titles has he won?

    a) 6

    b) 8

    c) 10

    d) 12

3. In which year did Roger Federer achieve his first Grand Slam victory?

    a) 2001

    b) 2003

    c) 2005

d) 2007

4. How many Australian Open singles titles has Federer won?

a) 3

b) 5

c) 6

d) 8

5. Federer completed the Career Grand Slam by winning which Grand Slam tournament?

a) French Open

b) Wimbledon

c) US Open

d) Australian Open

6. In which year did Federer achieve the Career Grand Slam?

a) 2006

b) 2009

c) 2012

d) 2017

7. Federer has won the ATP Tour Finals (formerly known as the Masters Cup) how many times?

    a) 4

    b) 6

    c) 8

    d) 10

8. How many times has Federer reached the final of the US Open?

    a) 6

    b) 7

    c) 8

    d) 9

9. Federer has an Olympic gold medal in which category?

    a) Singles

    b) Doubles

    c) Mixed Doubles

    d) Team Event

10. In which year did Federer win his first Olympic gold medal?

   a) 2004

   b) 2008

   c) 2012

   d) 2016

11. How many times has Federer been ranked as the World No. 1 in men's singles tennis?

   a) 272 weeks

   b) 310 weeks

   c) 360 weeks

   d) 412 weeks

12. Federer holds the record for the most consecutive weeks as World No. 1. How many consecutive weeks did he hold this position?

   a) 237 weeks

   b) 286 weeks

   c) 302 weeks

   d) 350 weeks

13. How many times has Federer won the Laureus World Sportsman of the Year award?

   a) 3

   b) 5

   c) 7

   d) 9

14. Federer has won how many Davis Cup titles with the Swiss team?

   a) 1

   b) 2

   c) 3

   d) 4

15. In which year did Federer achieve a calendar-year Grand Slam in men's doubles with Stan Wawrinka?

   a) 2008

   b) 2009

   c) 2010

   d) 2014

16. How many ATP Tour singles titles has Federer won in his career?

a) 95

b) 103

c) 112

d) 120

17. Federer won his 100th ATP Tour singles title in which city?

a) Dubai

b) Miami

c) Halle

d) Basel

18. How many times has Federer won the Stefan Edberg Sportsmanship Award?

a) 8

b) 10

c) 12

d) 14

19. Federer has a record streak of consecutive Grand Slam appearances. How many consecutive Grand Slam tournaments did he play?

    a) 65

    b) 75

    c) 85

    d) 95

20. In which year did Federer win his first ATP singles title?

    a) 1998

    b) 2000

    c) 2002

    d) 2004

21. Federer has won how many ATP 500 series titles?

    a) 10

    b) 15

    c) 20

    d) 25

22. How many times has Federer won the Pete Sampras Trophy for finishing the year as the World No. 1?

  a) 3

  b) 5

  c) 6

  d) 7

23. In which year did Federer win his last Grand Slam title as of 2022?

  a) 2016

  b) 2017

  c) 2018

  d) 2019

24. Federer has a positive head-to-head record against most of his rivals. Against which player has he struggled the most?

  a) Rafael Nadal

  b) Novak Djokovic

  c) Andy Murray

  d) Stan Wawrinka

25. How many times has Federer reached the final of the ATP World Tour Masters 1000 series tournaments?

a) 40

b) 45

c) 50

d) 55

26. Federer has won how many Grand Slam doubles titles in his career?

a) 1

b) 2

c) 3

d) 4

27. In which year did Federer win his first Laureus Sports Award?

a) 2004

b) 2006

c) 2008

d) 2010

28. How many times has Federer won the Arthur Ashe Humanitarian Award?

    a) 1

    b) 2

    c) 3

    d) 4

29. Federer won his first Grand Slam title at which tournament?

    a) Australian Open

    b) French Open

    c) Wimbledon

    d) US Open

30. How many times has Federer won the ATP Comeback Player of the Year award?

    a) 1

    b) 2

    c) 3

    d) 4

ANSWERS

1. b) 20

2. b) 8

3. b) 2003

4. c) 6

5. a) French Open

6. b) 2009

7. c) 6

8. b) 7

9. c) Mixed Doubles

10. b) 2008

11. c) 360 weeks

12. a) 237 weeks

13. a) 3

14. c) 3

15. d) 2014

16. b) 103

17. a) Dubai

18. d) 14

19. a) 65

20. b) 2000

21. c) 20

22. c) 6

23. c) 2018

24. b) Novak Djokovic

25. b) 45

26. a) 1

27. b) 2006

28. a) 1

29. c) Wimbledon

30. a) 1

PLAYING STYLE
QUESTION TIME!

1. What is Roger Federer's dominant hand for playing tennis?

   a) Left

   b) Right

2. Federer is known for his elegant one-handed backhand. What other player is often praised for a similar shot?

   a) Rafael Nadal

   b) Novak Djokovic

   c) Stan Wawrinka

   d) Andy Murray

3. What surface is considered to be Federer's favorite and where he has achieved the most success?

   a) Clay

   b) Grass

   c) Hardcourt

   d) Carpet

4. Federer is known for his exceptional movement on the court. Which term is often used to describe his graceful footwork?

   a) Swift Steps

   b) Cat-like Agility

   c) Powerful Strides

   d) Dynamic Footwork

5. Federer is recognized for his versatility on different surfaces. Which Grand Slam tournament is played on grass courts?

   a) Australian Open

   b) French Open

   c) Wimbledon

   d) US Open

6. What is Federer's preferred strategy when approaching the net during a match?

   a) Serve and Volley

   b) Aggressive Baseliner

   c) Counterpuncher

   d) Defensive Specialist

7. Federer is known for his ability to hit winners from difficult positions. What is this skill often referred to as?

a) Inside-out Forehand

b) Running Backhand

c) Down-the-line Shot

d) Off-balance Winner

8. Federer's serve is a crucial part of his game. What type of serve is he particularly known for?

a) Kick Serve

b) Slice Serve

c) Flat Serve

d) Topspin Serve

9. What is Federer's playing style often described as?

a) Power Baseline

b) Serve-and-Volley

c) Counterpuncher

d) Defensive Specialist

10. Federer has a signature shot known as the "SABR." What does SABR stand for?

a) Swift Attack Backhand Return

b) Sneaky Attack by Roger

c) Sudden Attack, Bold Return

d) Sneak Attack By Roger

11. Federer's forehand is known for its:

a) Topspin

b) Flat trajectory

c) Slice

d) Underhand Spin

12. Federer has a unique way of approaching and executing volleys. What is this style often referred to as?

a) Chip and Charge

b) Feather-touch Volley

c) Elegant Volleying

d) Swiss Precision

13. In crucial moments, Federer is known to rely on which shot to gain control of the point?

a) Drop Shot

b) Lob

c) Passing Shot

d) Overhead Smash

14. Federer is renowned for his ability to control the pace of the game. What term is often used to describe this skill?

a) Court Craft

b) Point Mastery

c) Ball Control

d) Shot Dictation

15. What is the nickname often used for Federer's playing style, emphasizing his all-around skills?

a) The Slicer

b) The Magician

c) The Powerhouse

d) The Acrobat

16. Federer's backhand is often praised for its:

a) Power

b) Consistency

c) Aggressiveness

d) Elegance

17. In tight situations, Federer is known for his calm and composed demeanor. What term is used to describe this aspect of his mental game?

a) Mental Fortitude

b) Zen Mode

c) Stoic Presence

d) Cool Composure

18. Federer has a unique skill in returning serve, often making it difficult for opponents. What is this skill called?

a) Quick Return

b) Blitz Return

c) Chip and Charge

d) Aggressive Return

19. Federer's drop shot is often referred to as:

a) The Slicer

b) The Dasher

c) The Whisper

d) The SABR

20. Federer is known to take risks with his shots, especially in critical moments. What term is often used to describe this aggressive style?

a) High-risk Tennis

b) All-out Attack

c) Fearless Play

d) Bold Tennis

21. What is Federer's preferred grip for his forehand shot?

a) Eastern Grip

b) Western Grip

c) Semi-western Grip

d) Continental Grip

22. Federer's game often involves using his opponent's pace against them. What term describes this tactic?

a) Counterpunching

b) Redirecting

c) Defensive Counter

d) Opponent Exploitation

23. Federer is known for his ability to vary the pace and spin of his shots. What term is often used to describe this tactic?

a) Shot Diversity

b) Spin Mastery

c) Ball Manipulation

d) Pace Control

24. What is the name of the shot where Federer charges forward after hitting a return to catch opponents off guard?

a) SABR

b) Chip and Charge

c) Sneak Attack

d) Net Rush

25. Federer's backhand slice is often used to:

a) Generate Power

b) Add Topspin

c) Change the Pace

d) Execute Drop Shots

26. Federer's serve-and-volley game is particularly effective on:

a) Grass Courts

b) Clay Courts

c) Hardcourts

d) Indoor Courts

27. Federer's movement on the court is often described as:

a) Agile and Graceful

b) Quick and Aggressive

c) Powerful and Forceful

d) Robotic and Precise

28. What is the term used for Federer's ability to hit the ball early and take it on the rise?

a) Early Attack

b) Quick Strike

c) First Strike Tennis

d) Pounce and Hit

29. Federer's approach to net play is often associated with:

a) Defensive Net Play

b) Aggressive Net Play

c) Net Retrieval

d) Net Chess

30. Federer is known for his on-the-run forehand winners. What term is often used to describe this skill?

a) Stretch Forehand

b) Dynamic Forehand

c) Running Forehand

d) Forehand Flash

ANSWERS

1. b) Right

2. c) Stan Wawrinka

3. b) Grass

4. b) Cat-like Agility

5. c) Wimbledon

6. a) Serve and Volley

7. d) Off-balance Winner

8. c) Flat Serve

9. b) Serve-and-Volley

10. c) Sudden Attack, Bold Return

11. b) Flat trajectory

12. c) Elegant Volleying

13. a) Drop Shot

14. c) Ball Control

15. b) The Magician

16. d) Elegance

17. a) Mental Fortitude

18. c) Chip and Charge

19. c) The Whisper

20. a) High-risk Tennis

21. c) Semi-western Grip

22. b) Redirecting

23. c) Ball Manipulation

24. a) SABR

25. c) Change the Pace

26. a) Grass Courts

27. a) Agile and Graceful

28. c) First Strike Tennis

29. b) Aggressive Net Play

30. c) Running Forehand

RIVALRIES
QUESTION TIME!

1. Federer's intense rivalry with which player is often considered one of the greatest in tennis history?

   a) Rafael Nadal

   b) Novak Djokovic

   c) Andy Murray

   d) Pete Sampras

2. The rivalry between Federer and Rafael Nadal is commonly referred to as:

   a) Fedal

   b) Rogal

   c) Rofed

   d) Rodal

3. Federer and Nadal have faced each other in the final of which Grand Slam tournament the most times?

   a) Australian Open

   b) French Open

c) Wimbledon

d) US Open

4. In the 2008 Wimbledon final, Federer lost to Nadal in a match often described as:

a) The Marathon Match

b) The Perfect Final

c) The Clash of Titans

d) The Battle of Legends

5. Federer and Novak Djokovic have had epic battles, including a memorable encounter at which Grand Slam final?

a) Australian Open

b) French Open

c) Wimbledon

d) US Open

6. Federer and Djokovic played in the longest Wimbledon final in history in:

a) 2017

b) 2018

c) 2019

d) 2020

7. The Federer-Nadal-Djokovic rivalry is often referred to as the:

a) Big Three

b) Grand Slam Trio

c) Power Trio

d) Tennis Titans

8. Federer has had a longstanding rivalry with which British player?

a) Andy Murray

b) Tim Henman

c) Greg Rusedski

d) Kyle Edmund

9. Federer and Murray faced off in the final of which Grand Slam tournament?

a) Australian Open

b) French Open

c) Wimbledon

d) US Open

10. In the 2012 Wimbledon final, Federer defeated Murray to secure his:

    a) 16th Grand Slam title

    b) 17th Grand Slam title

    c) 18th Grand Slam title

    d) 19th Grand Slam title

11. Federer's rivalry with Andy Roddick peaked in the Wimbledon final of:

    a) 2003

    b) 2006

    c) 2009

    d) 2012

12. In the 2009 Wimbledon final, Federer defeated Roddick in a match often remembered for:

    a) A Golden Set

    b) A Rain Delay

    c) Multiple Tiebreaks

    d) A Marathon Fifth Set

13. Federer has had a notable rivalry with Juan Martin del Potro, who defeated him in the final of which Grand Slam tournament?

a) Australian Open

b) French Open

c) Wimbledon

d) US Open

14. In the 2009 US Open final, Federer lost to del Potro in a match known for its:

a) Five-set Drama

b) Quick Finish

c) Marathon Tiebreak

d) Rain Interruption

15. Federer and Stan Wawrinka have had a rivalry that often surfaces in matches between:

a) Davis Cup

b) Olympic Games

c) ATP Finals

d) Grand Slam Tournaments

16. Federer and Wawrinka faced off in an all-Swiss final at which Grand Slam tournament?

   a) Australian Open

   b) French Open

   c) Wimbledon

   d) US Open

17. The Federer-Wawrinka rivalry is sometimes referred to as the:

   a) Swiss Showdown

   b) Alpine Duel

   c) Swiss Slam

   d) Helvetic Clash

18. Federer has faced off against which player in multiple Olympic Games finals?

   a) Rafael Nadal

   b) Novak Djokovic

   c) Andy Murray

   d) Juan Martin del Potro

19. Federer and Djokovic had a memorable rivalry in the semifinals of which Grand Slam tournament in 2011?

a) Australian Open

b) French Open

c) Wimbledon

d) US Open

20. Federer and Djokovic played in the final of which ATP Tour Finals edition?

a) 2012

b) 2014

c) 2015

d) 2018

21. Federer has had a rivalry with Lleyton Hewitt, whom he faced in the final of which Grand Slam tournament in 2004?

a) Australian Open

b) French Open

c) Wimbledon

d) US Open

22. The Federer-Hewitt rivalry is sometimes referred to as the:

a) Maestro vs. Rocket

b) Swiss Surge

c) Wizard Duel

d) Grass Confrontation

23. Federer has faced off against Marat Safin in the final of which Grand Slam tournament?

a) Australian Open

b) French Open

c) Wimbledon

d) US Open

24. In the 2004 Australian Open final, Federer lost to Safin in a match remembered for its:

a) Quick Finish

b) Epic Length

c) Tiebreak Drama

d) Rain Interruption

25. Federer and Agassi had a rivalry in the early 2000s, with notable matches at which Grand Slam tournament?

  a) Australian Open

  b) French Open

  c) Wimbledon

  d) US Open

26. The Federer-Agassi rivalry is sometimes referred to as the:

  a) Swiss-American Clash

  b) Maestro vs. Veteran

  c) Elegant Encounter

  d) Generational Duel

27. Federer and David Nalbandian had a rivalry that often featured matches in the final of which tournament?

  a) Wimbledon

  b) ATP Tour Finals

  c) US Open

  d) Davis Cup

28. In the 2005 ATP Tour Finals, Federer lost to Nalbandian in a match remembered for its:

a) Marathon Tiebreak

b) Comeback Victory

c) Quick Finish

d) Rain Interruption

29. Federer and Nikolay Davydenko had a rivalry with notable matches at which tournament?

a) Australian Open

b) French Open

c) Wimbledon

d) US Open

30. In the 2009 ATP Tour Finals, Federer defeated Davydenko in a match remembered for its:

a) Marathon Tiebreak

b) Three-set Thriller

c) Quick Finish

d) Championship Point Save

ANSWERS

1. a) Rafael Nadal

2. a) Fedal

3. c) Wimbledon

4. a) The Marathon Match

5. c) Wimbledon

6. b) 2018

7. a) Big Three

8. a) Andy Murray

9. c) Wimbledon

10. b) 17th Grand Slam title

11. c) 2009

12. d) A Marathon Fifth Set

13. d) US Open

14. a) Five-set Drama

15. a) Davis Cup

16. a) Australian Open

17. a) Swiss Showdown

18. d) Juan Martin del Potro

19. c) Wimbledon

20. c) 2015

21. c) Wimbledon

22. a) Maestro vs. Rocket

23. a) Australian Open

24. b) Epic Length

25. a) Australian Open

26. b) Maestro vs. Veteran

27. b) ATP Tour Finals

28. b) Comeback Victory

29. b) French Open

30. d) Championship Point Save

OFF COURT PERSONA

QUESTION TIME!

1. Roger Federer was born in which country?

   a) France

   b) Switzerland

   c) Sweden

   d) Germany

2. Federer is fluent in how many languages?

   a) 1

   b) 2

   c) 3

   d) 4

3. What is the name of Roger Federer's wife?

   a) Mirka

   b) Anna

   c) Maria

d) Lara

4. How many children does Roger Federer have?

   a) 1

   b) 2

   c) 3

   d) 4

5. Federer established the Roger Federer Foundation to support education in which region?

   a) Europe

   b) Africa

   c) Asia

   d) North America

6. In 2003, Federer was appointed as a UNICEF Goodwill Ambassador. What cause does UNICEF primarily focus on?

   a) Education

   b) Healthcare

   c) Poverty

   d) Child Welfare

7. Federer is known for his philanthropy. Which of the following initiatives did he launch to support education?

   a) Match for Unity

   b) Serve for Good

   c) Rally for Relief

   d) Aces for Change

8. Federer has won the prestigious Laureus Sportsman of the Year award how many times?

   a) 2

   b) 4

   c) 6

   d) 8

9. What is the name of Roger Federer's autobiography, published in 2021?

   a) "The Champion Within"

   b) "My Story: Roger Federer"

   c) "Roger's Odyssey"

   d) "On the Court and Beyond"

10. Federer has been known for his sportsmanship. How many Stefan Edberg Sportsmanship Awards has he won?

a) 8

b) 10

c) 12

d) 14

11. Roger Federer's signature logo includes his initials "RF" and:

a) A tennis racket

b) A crown

c) A globe

d) An eagle

12. In 2006, Federer became the first living person to have a coin minted in his honor in which country?

a) Switzerland

b) France

c) United States

d) Australia

13. Federer is associated with a luxury Swiss watch brand. Which brand is it?

a) Rolex

b) Omega

c) Patek Philippe

d) Audemars Piguet

14. What is the title of the children's book co-authored by Roger Federer?

a) "Roger and Friends"

b) "Federer's Adventures"

c) "The Magic of Tennis"

d) "Hey, Roger!"

15. Federer's involvement in the "Match for Africa" events aims to raise funds for:

a) Cancer Research

b) Education Initiatives

c) Environmental Conservation

d) Humanitarian Aid

16. In 2020, Federer was named the first global ambassador for which clothing brand?

a) Nike

b) Adidas

c) Uniqlo

d) Lacoste

17. Federer has a line of tennis equipment and apparel with which sports brand?

a) Nike

b) Wilson

c) Adidas

d) Head

18. Federer is known for his interest in art. In 2019, he auctioned his collection for charity. Which charity did the proceeds go to?

a) UNICEF

b) Roger Federer Foundation

c) Red Cross

d) Save the Children

19. What is the name of the South African player with whom Federer played the "Match in Africa 6" in 2020?

a) Kevin Anderson

b) Lloyd Harris

c) Raven Klaasen

d) Lucas Sithole

20. Federer's social media presence is notable. Which platform does he use most frequently to connect with fans?

a) Instagram

b) Twitter

c) Facebook

d) TikTok

21. Federer has been involved in promoting which global event that encourages physical activity and sports participation?

a) International Yoga Day

b) Global Running Day

c) World Health Day

d) Olympic Day

22. Federer often collaborates with a famous tennis player and friend to create humorous social media content. Who is this player?

a) Rafael Nadal

b) Novak Djokovic

c) Andy Murray

d) Stan Wawrinka

23. Federer is known for his classic and stylish on-court attire. Which fashion house has he collaborated with for his tennis outfits?

a) Gucci

b) Louis Vuitton

c) Ralph Lauren

d) Chanel

24. What is the name of Federer's signature fragrance line?

a) RF Essence

b) Maestro Musk

c) Grand Slam Aroma

d) Perfection Parfum

25. Federer's off-court hobbies include playing which musical instrument?

a) Piano

b) Guitar

c) Violin

d) Flute

26. Roger Federer is associated with a famous chocolate brand in Switzerland. What is the name of the brand?

a) Toblerone

b) Lindt

c) Nestle

d) Milka

27. Federer has a street named after him in which Swiss city?

a) Zurich

b) Basel

c) Geneva

d) Bern

28. In 2018, Federer became the first living Swiss to have a:

a) Stadium named after him

b) Statue erected in his honor

c) Banknote featuring his image

d) Mountain named after him

29. Federer has a charitable partnership with which footwear brand to provide education for children in Africa?

a) Nike

b) Adidas

c) Puma

d) TOMS

30. Roger Federer's parents are of Swiss and:

a) French

b) German

c) Italian

d) Spanish

ANSWERS

1. b) Switzerland

2. c) 3

3. a) Mirka

4. c) 3

5. b) Africa

6. a) Education

7. d) Aces for Change

8. c) 6

9. b) "My Story: Roger Federer"

10. d) 14

11. b) A crown

12. a) Switzerland

13. b) Omega

14. a) "Roger and Friends"

15. b) Education Initiatives

16. c) Uniqlo

17. b) Wilson

18. b) Roger Federer Foundation

19. b) Lloyd Harris

20. b) Twitter

21. b) Global Running Day

22. c) Andy Murray

23. c) Ralph Lauren

24. a) RF Essence

25. b) Guitar

26. b) Lindt

27. b) Basel

28. c) Banknote featuring his image

29. d) TOMS

30. a) French

CHARITABLE CONTRIBUTIONS
QUESTION TIME!

1. Roger Federer established the Roger Federer Foundation in:

   a) 2001

   b) 2004

   c) 2006

   d) 2008

2. The primary focus of the Roger Federer Foundation is to support:

   a) Healthcare

   b) Sports Development

   c) Education

   d) Environmental Conservation

3. In which continent does the Roger Federer Foundation primarily operate?

   a) Europe

   b) North America

c) Africa

d) Asia

4. The foundation aims to provide quality education to children in which age group?

a) Preschool

b) Primary School

c) High School

d) College

5. Federer's foundation believes in the transformative power of education to empower children to become:

a) Athletes

b) Leaders

c) Artists

d) Scientists

6. The Roger Federer Foundation has launched projects in several African countries. Which of the following is one of them?

a) Switzerland

b) Kenya

c) Germany

d) Japan

7. The foundation collaborates with local organizations to implement its education initiatives. What is the key principle of these collaborations?

a) Short-term Impact

b) Long-term Sustainability

c) Immediate Results

d) Independent Operation

8. Federer's foundation is committed to addressing educational challenges related to:

a) Language Barriers

b) Lack of Infrastructure

c) Gender Inequality

d) All of the Above

9. The Roger Federer Foundation believes in providing education as a means to break the cycle of:

a) Poverty

b) Disease

c) Ignorance

d) Corruption

10. In addition to education, the foundation also supports programs related to:

a) Sports

b) Healthcare

c) Environmental Conservation

d) Art and Culture

11. The foundation's projects often emphasize creating a conducive learning environment through:

a) Building Schools

b) Providing School Supplies

c) Teacher Training

d) All of the Above

12. Federer's foundation collaborated with Credit Suisse to launch a program aimed at addressing education challenges in:

a) India

b) South America

c) Sub-Saharan Africa

d) Southeast Asia

13. The "Swiss Indoors for Africa" is an initiative by Federer to raise funds for his foundation through:

a) Tennis Exhibitions

b) Charity Auctions

c) Ticket Sales

d) Corporate Sponsorships

14. Federer has hosted charity matches called "Match for Africa." The proceeds from these matches go towards:

a) Medical Research

b) Education Initiatives

c) Environmental Protection

d) Humanitarian Aid

15. In 2018, the Roger Federer Foundation reached a milestone by reaching how many million children with its education programs?

a) 1 million

b) 5 million

c) 10 million

d) 15 million

16. Federer's foundation aims to foster a learning environment that encourages:

a) Competition

b) Collaboration

c) Individualism

d) Rote Learning

17. The foundation's commitment to gender equality is reflected in its efforts to ensure equal access to education for:

a) Boys only

b) Girls only

c) Both Boys and Girls

d) Privileged Children

18. In 2019, Federer played a charity match in Cape Town, South Africa, called the "Match in Africa." What was the main objective of this event?

a) Raise Funds for Education

b) Promote Tennis in Africa

c) Address Climate Change

d) Combat Infectious Diseases

19. The "Match in Africa" event in 2020 featured a doubles match with Federer partnering with which international celebrity?

a) Bill Gates

b) Elon Musk

c) Leonardo DiCaprio

d) Oprah Winfrey

20. The Roger Federer Foundation actively supports the United Nations' Sustainable Development Goal related to:

a) Quality Education

b) Clean Water and Sanitation

c) Affordable and Clean Energy

d) Zero Hunger

21. Federer's foundation focuses on providing education to children in challenging socio-economic conditions, including those affected by:

a) Armed Conflicts

b) Natural Disasters

c) Economic Inequality

d) All of the Above

22. The foundation's commitment to long-term impact is evident in its:

a) Short-term Projects

b) One-time Donations

c) Multi-year Programs

d) Seasonal Campaigns

23. Federer's involvement in charity extends beyond his foundation. In 2020, he donated masks and provided support during the COVID-19 pandemic in which country?

a) Switzerland

b) United States

c) China

d) Brazil

24. In 2016, Federer auctioned his custom-designed tennis racquet to support education projects. What was the theme of the racquet design?

a) Swiss Alps

b) African Safari

c) Space Exploration

d) Ocean Conservation

25. The Roger Federer Foundation's philosophy is grounded in the belief that education empowers children to become responsible and:

a) Independent

b) Wealthy

c) Famous

d) Powerful

26. Federer's commitment to education has earned him recognition as a UNESCO:

a) Goodwill Ambassador

b) Advocate for Children

c) Champion of Youth

d) Ambassador for Peace

27. In addition to the "Match in Africa" events, Federer has collaborated with other tennis players to organize charity

matches. Who is his frequent partner in these events?

a) Rafael Nadal

b) Novak Djokovic

c) Andy Murray

d) Stan Wawrinka

28. Federer's foundation emphasizes the importance of education in fostering:

a) Cultural Diversity

b) Social Harmony

c) Economic Growth

d) Global Citizenship

29. Federer's commitment to education aligns with his belief that every child deserves the opportunity to:

a) Play Tennis

b) Pursue Their Dreams

c) Travel the World

d) Become a Professional Athlete

30. The Roger Federer Foundation envisions a world where education empowers children to overcome barriers and realize their:

a) Academic Potential

b) Sporting Talent

c) Artistic Abilities

d) Full Potential

ANSWERS

1. b) 2004

2. c) Education

3. c) Africa

4. b) Primary School

5. b) Leaders

6. b) Kenya

7. b) Long-term Sustainability

8. d) All of the Above

9. a) Poverty

10. c) Environmental Conservation

11. d) All of the Above

12. c) Sub-Saharan Africa

13. b) Charity Auctions

14. b) Education Initiatives

15. c) 10 million

16. b) Collaboration

17. c) Both Boys and Girls

18. a) Raise Funds for Education

19. a) Bill Gates

20. a) Quality Education

21. d) All of the Above

22. c) Multi-year Programs

23. a) Switzerland

24. b) African Safari

25. a) Independent

26. a) Goodwill Ambassador

27. a) Rafael Nadal

28. b) Social Harmony

29. b) Pursue Their Dreams

30. d) Full Potential

MEDIA AND PUBLIC IMAGE

QUESTION TIME!

1. Roger Federer is often referred to as the:

a) King of Clay

b) Maestro

c) Djoker

d) Swiss Sensation

2. Federer has been featured on the cover of which prominent sports magazine multiple times?

a) Sports Illustrated

b) ESPN The Magazine

c) GQ

d) TIME

3. Federer has a reputation for his on-court elegance and sportsmanship. Which prestigious award has he won a record number of times for sportsmanship?

a) ATP Player of the Year

b) Stefan Edberg Sportsmanship Award

c) Laureus Sportsman of the Year

d) Olympic Sportsmanship Medal

4. Federer has a signature logo that combines his initials "RF" with:

a) A tennis racket

b) A crown

c) A globe

d) A lion

5. Federer has been praised for his philanthropic efforts. Which magazine named him one of the most charitable athletes?

a) Forbes

b) TIME

c) GQ

d) Vanity Fair

6. Federer has been an ambassador for which luxury Swiss watch brand since 2004?

a) Rolex

b) Omega

c) Patek Philippe

d) Hublot

7. Federer is known for his calm demeanor on and off the court. What nickname is often associated with his composed on-court presence?

a) Ice Man

b) Firebrand

c) Thunderbolt

d) Hurricane

8. Federer's media and public image are often characterized by:

a) Flamboyance

b) Stoicism

c) Aggressiveness

d) Eccentricity

9. Federer has a strong social media presence. On which platform does he frequently share updates with fans?

a) Instagram

b) Twitter

c) Facebook

d) TikTok

10. Federer has been involved in humorous social media content, including collaborations with which fellow tennis player?

a) Rafael Nadal

b) Novak Djokovic

c) Andy Murray

d) Stan Wawrinka

11. Federer's stylish on-court attire has been designed by the fashion house:

a) Gucci

b) Louis Vuitton

c) Uniqlo

d) Nike

12. Federer has a street named after him in which Swiss city?

a) Zurich

b) Basel

c) Geneva

d) Bern

13. In 2018, Federer became the first living Swiss to have a:

a) Stadium named after him

b) Statue erected in his honor

c) Banknote featuring his image

d) Mountain named after him

14. Federer's endorsements include partnerships with global brands such as:

a) Coca-Cola

b) Pepsi

c) Red Bull

d) Starbucks

15. Federer has been featured in advertisements for which iconic sports shoe brand?

a) Nike

b) Adidas

c) Puma

d) New Balance

16. Federer has been praised for his ability to engage with the media and fans in multiple languages. How many languages is he fluent in?

a) 1

b) 2

c) 3

d) 4

17. Federer has expressed his passion for which sport other than tennis, leading to his involvement in its promotion and development?

a) Golf

b) Soccer

c) Basketball

d) Skiing

18. Federer's off-court persona is often characterized by his:

a) Extravagance

b) Humility

c) Eccentricity

d) Aloofness

19. Federer has been associated with a famous chocolate brand in Switzerland. What is the name of the brand?

a) Toblerone

b) Lindt

c) Nestle

d) Milka

20. In 2020, Federer appeared in a documentary titled:

a) "Unraveled Legacy"

b) "Strokes of Greatness"

c) "Being Federer"

d) "The Roger Effect"

21. Federer's media interviews often highlight his:

a) Competitive Edge

b) Philosophical Insights

c) Controversial Statements

d) Emotional Vulnerability

22. Federer has been associated with a famous credit card company. Which one is it?

a) Visa

b) MasterCard

c) American Express

d) Discover

23. Federer's demeanor on the court, often staying calm under pressure, has earned him the nickname:

a) The Ice Man

b) The Firebrand

c) The Gentleman

d) The Magician

24. Federer's endorsement deals extend beyond sports. He has been associated with which high-end automobile brand?

a) Mercedes-Benz

b) Ferrari

c) Porsche

d) BMW

25. Federer's media image is often characterized by a combination of:

a) Elegance and Grace

b) Power and Aggression

c) Flamboyance and Extravagance

d) Stoicism and Composure

26. Federer has been featured in a coffee table book titled:

a) "Federer: A Legend Unleashed"

b) "The Maestro's Magic"

c) "Roger Federer: Style and Grace"

d) "Timeless Elegance"

27. Federer has a wax statue at which famous wax museum?

a) Madame Tussauds

b) Grevin Wax Museum

c) Hollywood Wax Museum

d) National Wax Museum

28. Federer's media image is often associated with:

a) Fashion Faux Pas

b) Graceful Elegance

c) Outspoken Opinions

d) Unconventional Styles

29. Federer has participated in which tennis exhibition event known for its casual and entertaining format?

a) Davis Cup

b) Laver Cup

c) Hopman Cup

d) Kooyong Classic

30. Federer's media and public image contribute to his legacy as not just a tennis player but also as:

a) a Cultural Icon

b) a Business Mogul

c) a Political Figure

d) an Environmental Activist

ANSWERS

1. b) Maestro

2. b) ESPN The Magazine

3. b) Stefan Edberg Sportsmanship Award

4. b) A crown

5. a) Forbes

6. a) Rolex

7. a) Ice Man

8. b) Stoicism

9. a) Instagram

10. c) Andy Murray

11. c) Uniqlo

12. b) Basel

13. c) Banknote featuring his image

14. c) Red Bull

15. a) Nike

16. c) 3

17. b) Soccer

18. b) Humility

19. b) Lindt

20. b) "Strokes of Greatness"

21. b) Philosophical Insights

22. c) American Express

23. a) The Ice Man

24. c) Porsche

25. a) Elegance and Grace

26. c) "Roger Federer: Style and Grace"

27. a) Madame Tussauds

28. b) Graceful Elegance

29. b) Laver Cup

30. a) a Cultural Icon

TRAINING AND FITNESS
QUESTION TIME!

1. What is Roger Federer's preferred surface for tennis?

   a. Clay

   b. Grass

   c. Hardcourt

   d. Carpet

2. Which of the following Grand Slam tournaments has Roger Federer won the most times?

   a. Australian Open

   b. French Open

   c. Wimbledon

   d. US Open

3. What is Roger Federer's usual racquet brand?

   a. Wilson

b. Head

c. Babolat

d. Yonex

4. In which year did Roger Federer turn professional?

a. 1996

b. 1998

c. 2000

d. 2002

5. What is the nickname often used for Roger Federer?

a. The King

b. The Rocket

c. The Maestro

d. The Beast

6. Which country does Roger Federer represent in international competitions?

a. United States

b. Switzerland

c. Australia

d. Spain

7. What is Roger Federer's dominant hand in tennis?

a. Right

b. Left

8. In which year did Roger Federer win his first Grand Slam title?

a. 2001

b. 2003

c. 2005

d. 2007

9. What is the signature shot of Roger Federer?

a. Forehand

b. Backhand

c. Serve

d. Volley

10. Which fitness component is crucial for endurance in tennis?

a. Strength

b. Flexibility

c. Cardiovascular endurance

d. Speed

11. What is the role of agility in tennis?

a. Powerful serves

b. Quick lateral movements

c. High jumps

d. Long-distance running

12. Which type of training helps improve muscular strength for a tennis player like Roger Federer?

a. Pilates

b. Yoga

c. Weight training

d. Aerobic exercise

13. What type of footwear is commonly used in tennis to provide stability and support during lateral movements?

a. Running shoes

b. Basketball shoes

c. Cross-training shoes

d. Tennis shoes

14. Which of the following is an example of a dynamic warm-up exercise suitable for tennis players?

a. Static stretching

b. Jumping jacks

c. Holding a plank

d. Deep breathing exercises

15. What is the importance of core strength in tennis?

a. Enhanced speed

b. Improved balance and stability

c. Powerful serves

d. Long-distance running ability

16. Which nutrient is essential for muscle recovery and repair after intense training sessions?

a. Carbohydrates

b. Protein

c. Fat

d. Vitamins

17. What is the purpose of interval training in a tennis player's fitness routine?

a. Building endurance

b. Increasing flexibility

c. Enhancing explosive power

d. Improving coordination

18. Which of the following is a common strategy in Roger Federer's training routine to prevent injuries?

a. Overtraining

b. Adequate rest and recovery

c. Ignoring warm-up exercises

d. Heavy reliance on supplements

19. What role does mental conditioning play in Roger Federer's training?

a. Negligible impact

b. Primary focus

c. Secondary consideration

d. Occasional emphasis

20. Which aspect of fitness is particularly important for executing precise and controlled shots in tennis?

a. Power

b. Coordination

c. Speed

d. Flexibility

21. What is the purpose of cross-training in Roger Federer's fitness regimen?

a. Specialization in one type of exercise

b. Avoiding variety in workouts

c. Preventing burnout and injury

d. Maximizing rest days

22. How does Roger Federer incorporate flexibility training into his routine?

a. Static stretching

b. Heavy weightlifting

c. High-intensity interval training

d. Agility drills

23. What is the importance of proper hydration for a tennis player like Roger Federer?

    a. Enhancing muscle strength

    b. Preventing cramps and fatigue

    c. Boosting speed

    d. Increasing reaction time

24. Which of the following factors contributes to Roger Federer's longevity in professional tennis?

    a. Inadequate rest

    b. Strict adherence to a single training method

    c. Well-managed workload and recovery

    d. Lack of mental resilience

25. What is the recommended ratio of work to rest in interval training for tennis players?

    a. 1:1

    b. 2:1

    c. 3:1

    d. 4:1

26. How does Roger Federer maintain his mental focus during matches?

    a. Ignoring opponents' strategies

    b. Meditation and visualization

    c. Avoiding pre-match rituals

    d. Relying solely on physical preparation

27. What is the significance of balance training for tennis players?

    a. Reducing agility

    b. Enhancing control and stability

    c. Slowing down movements

    d. Negligible impact on performance

28. What type of recovery strategies are commonly used by Roger Federer after intense matches or training sessions?

    a. Ice baths and compression garments

    b. Ignoring recovery altogether

    c. Immediate return to regular training

    d. Excessive caffeine consumption

29. How does Roger Federer adapt his training routine to different playing surfaces?

a. Ignoring surface variations

b. Modifying movement patterns and strategies

c. Sticking to a rigid routine

d. Avoiding specific surfaces altogether

30. Which tournament did Roger Federer win in 2009 after a thrilling final against Andy Roddick that went to 16-14 in the fifth set?

a. Australian Open

b. French Open

c. Wimbledon

d. US Open

ANSWERS

1. b

2. c

3. a

4. b

5. c

6. b

7. a

8. b

9. a

10. c

11. b

12. c

13. d

14. b

15. b

16. b

17. c

18. b

19. b

20. b

21. c

22. a

23. b

24. c

25. b

26. b

27. b

28. a

29. b

30. c

LEGACY IN TENNIS

QUESTION TIME!

1. How many Grand Slam singles titles has Roger Federer won throughout his career?

    a. 16

    b. 20

    c. 23

    d. 27

2. Which Grand Slam tournament did Roger Federer win first in his career?

    a. Australian Open

    b. French Open

    c. Wimbledon

    d. US Open

3. In which year did Roger Federer achieve his first Grand Slam victory?

    a. 2000

    b. 2003

    c. 2006

d. 2009

4. How many consecutive weeks did Roger Federer hold the world No. 1 ranking, setting a record at that time?

a. 237

b. 286

c. 310

d. 365

5. Which player ended Roger Federer's record streak of consecutive Grand Slam semifinals appearances?

a. Rafael Nadal

b. Novak Djokovic

c. Andy Murray

d. Juan Martin del Potro

6. How many times has Roger Federer won the Laureus World Sportsman of the Year award?

a. 3

b. 5

c. 7

d. 9

7. What is the nickname often used to refer to Roger Federer due to his elegant playing style?

a. The Rocket

b. The Maestro

c. The Beast

d. The Powerhouse

8. Which year did Roger Federer complete the Career Grand Slam by winning the French Open?

a. 2005

b. 2007

c. 2009

d. 2012

9. Who did Roger Federer defeat in the longest Wimbledon final in history in 2019 to secure his 20th Grand Slam title?

a. Rafael Nadal

b. Novak Djokovic

c. Andy Murray

d. Marin Cilic

10. How many Olympic gold medals has Roger Federer won in his career?

a. 0

b. 1

c. 2

d. 3

11. Which player did Roger Federer defeat in the 2007 Australian Open final to clinch the title?

a. Rafael Nadal

b. Novak Djokovic

c. Andy Roddick

d. Marcos Baghdatis

12. In which year did Roger Federer achieve a "Golden Career Grand Slam" by winning each Grand Slam and an Olympic gold medal?

a. 2008

b. 2012

c. 2016

d. 2020

13. How many times has Roger Federer won the ATP Tour Finals title?

a. 3

b. 5

c. 6

d. 8

14. Who was Roger Federer's rival in many memorable Grand Slam finals, including the 2008 Wimbledon final often regarded as one of the greatest matches ever played?

a. Rafael Nadal

b. Novak Djokovic

c. Andy Murray

d. Juan Martin del Potro

15. What is the total number of weeks Roger Federer spent at the world No. 1 ranking as of his knowledge cutoff in January 2022?

a. 310

b. 325

c. 340

d. 365

16. Which Grand Slam tournament did Roger Federer skip in 2017 to focus on his preparation for the grass-court season?

a. Australian Open

b. French Open

c. Wimbledon

d. US Open

17. How many Wimbledon titles has Roger Federer won in his career?

a. 6

b. 8

c. 10

d. 12

18. Who did Roger Federer defeat in the 2018 Australian Open final to secure his 20th Grand Slam title?

a. Rafael Nadal

b. Novak Djokovic

c. Marin Cilic

d. Andy Murray

19. In 2017, Roger Federer became the oldest man in the Open Era to win a Grand Slam singles title at which tournament?

a. Australian Open

b. French Open

c. Wimbledon

d. US Open

20. How many times has Roger Federer won the BBC Overseas Sports Personality of the Year award?

a. 3

b. 5

c. 7

d. 9

21. Which record did Roger Federer set by reaching the 2017 Wimbledon final?

a. Oldest Wimbledon finalist in the Open Era

b. Fastest serve in Wimbledon history

c. Most aces in a single Wimbledon tournament

d. Longest winning streak at Wimbledon

22. Who did Roger Federer defeat in the 2009 French Open final to complete his Career Grand Slam?

a. Rafael Nadal

b. Novak Djokovic

c. Andy Murray

d. Robin Soderling

23. Which company has been Roger Federer's longtime clothing and apparel sponsor?

a. Nike

b. Adidas

c. Under Armour

d. Lacoste

24. How many times has Roger Federer won the Stefan Edberg Sportsmanship Award?

a. 5

b. 7

c. 9

d. 11

25. In which year did Roger Federer achieve a calendar-year Grand Slam in doubles, partnering with Stan Wawrinka at the Olympics?

a. 2004

b. 2008

c. 2012

d. 2016

26. What is the name of the charitable foundation founded by Roger Federer?

a. Federer Foundation

b. Roger's Relief

c. Tennis for Good

d. Swiss Philanthropy

27. How many times has Roger Federer won the ESPY Award for Best Male Tennis Player?

a. 5

b. 7

c. 9

d. 11

28. Which player has Roger Federer faced the most times in Grand Slam finals?

a. Rafael Nadal

b. Novak Djokovic

c. Andy Murray

d. Juan Martin del Potro

29. In 2021, Roger Federer withdrew from the French Open to prioritize his preparation for which Grand Slam tournament?

a. Australian Open

b. Wimbledon

c. US Open

d. None of the above

30. Which player did Roger Federer defeat in the 2004 Australian Open final to win his first hardcourt Grand Slam title?

a. Rafael Nadal

b. Marat Safin

c. Andy Roddick

d. Andre Agassi

ANSWERS

1. b

2. c

3. b

4. a

5. b

6. b

7. b

8. c

9. b

10. a

11. c

12. a

13. c

14. a

15. b

16. b

17. b

18. c

19. a

20. b

21. a

22. d

23. a

24. b

25. b

26. a

27. b

28. b

29. b

30. c

FAN BASE AND GLOBAL POPULARITY

QUESTION TIME!

1. Which country does Roger Federer hail from?

   a. United States

   b. Spain

   c. Switzerland

   d. Australia

2. What is the nickname commonly used for Roger Federer by his fans?

   a. The King

   b. The Flash

   c. The Warrior

   d. The Magician

3. Which social media platform is Roger Federer most active on, connecting with his global fan base?

   a. Instagram

   b. Twitter

c. Facebook

d. TikTok

4. In which year did Roger Federer establish the Roger Federer Foundation, contributing to his global popularity?

a. 2003

b. 2006

c. 2009

d. 2012

5. What is the name of the signature clothing line launched by Roger Federer in collaboration with a major sportswear brand?

a. RF Style

b. Federer Fashion

c. Nike Federer Collection

d. Uniqlo Roger Federer

6. Which famous Swiss watch brand has a long-standing partnership with Roger Federer, adding to his global appeal?

a. Rolex

b. Omega

c. Patek Philippe

d. Hublot

7. What unique aspect of Roger Federer's playing style has contributed to his popularity among tennis fans worldwide?

a. Powerful serves

b. Aggressive baseline play

c. Elegant and versatile game

d. Net-rushing tactics

8. Which major sports event did Roger Federer miss in 2020, causing disappointment among his global fan base?

a. Wimbledon

b. French Open

c. US Open

d. Australian Open

9. In which year did Roger Federer win the ATP Fan Favorite Award for the first time?

a. 2004

b. 2008

c. 2012

d. 2016

10. What is the significance of Roger Federer's iconic "RF" logo in building his brand and fan base?

a. It represents his favorite shot.

b. It stands for "Roger Federer."

c. It signifies his preferred playing surface.

d. It's a tribute to his hometown.

11. Which Grand Slam tournament has a nickname that pays homage to Roger Federer's playing style as the "King of Grass"?

a. Australian Open

b. French Open

c. Wimbledon

d. US Open

12. Which award did Roger Federer receive at the 2020 Laureus World Sports Awards, showcasing his impact beyond tennis?

a. Best Male Athlete

b. Sportsman of the Year

c. Lifetime Achievement Award

d. Philanthropist of the Year

13. What is the estimated net worth of Roger Federer, contributing to his status as one of the highest-paid athletes globally?

a. $100 million

b. $250 million

c. $500 million

d. $1 billion

14. Which global sports apparel brand signed a sponsorship deal with Roger Federer in 2018 after his contract with Nike ended?

a. Adidas

b. Puma

c. Under Armour

d. Uniqlo

15. How many times has Roger Federer won the ATP Stefan Edberg Sportsmanship Award, reflecting his conduct on and off the court?

    a. 5

    b. 7

    c. 9

    d. 11

16. In which year did Roger Federer surpass 20 million followers on Twitter, showcasing his extensive social media reach?

    a. 2010

    b. 2015

    c. 2018

    d. 2021

17. Which of Roger Federer's personal qualities is often praised by fans and contributes to his global popularity?

    a. Intimidating demeanor

    b. Humility and sportsmanship

    c. Aggressive playing style

d. Reserved and aloof personality

18. Which major fashion magazine featured Roger Federer on its cover, reflecting his influence beyond the sports world?

a. Vogue

b. GQ

c. Elle

d. Harper's Bazaar

19. What is the name of the charitable foundation founded by Roger Federer, engaging fans in philanthropy?

a. Federer's Angels

b. Tennis Cares

c. RF Love

d. Roger Federer Foundation

20. Which music genre is often associated with Roger Federer, showcasing his diverse interests and appealing to a wide fan base?

a. Pop

b. Classical

c. Hip-Hop

d. Rock

21. Which tournament did Roger Federer win in 2017, marking his return to competitive tennis after a brief hiatus and delighting his global fan base?

a. Australian Open

b. Wimbledon

c. US Open

d. Indian Wells Masters

22. What is the name of the documentary series released in 2020 that provides an intimate look into Roger Federer's life, increasing his global visibility?

a. "Federer Uncovered"

b. "Being Roger Federer"

c. "RF Revealed"

d. "The Roger Federer Chronicles"

23. Which social media platform did Roger Federer use to announce his comeback to professional tennis in 2021, exciting his fans globally?

a. Instagram

b. Twitter

c. Facebook

d. TikTok

24. Which city hosted "The Match in Africa," an exhibition match featuring Roger Federer and Rafael Nadal, drawing massive global attention?

a. Zurich

b. Cape Town

c. Paris

d. Tokyo

25. What is the name of the famous rivalry between Roger Federer and Rafael Nadal, capturing the imaginations of tennis fans worldwide?

a. Fedal Clash

b. Swiss-Spanish Showdown

c. Battle of the Titans

d. Rafa-Roger Rivalry

26. Which aspect of Roger Federer's game is often highlighted in marketing campaigns, contributing to his broader appeal beyond tennis enthusiasts?

a. Powerful serves

b. Graceful movement

c. Aggressive volleys

d. Strategic baseline play

27. Which magazine named Roger Federer as one of the "100 Most Influential People in the World" in 2018?

a. Time

b. Forbes

c. Vanity Fair

d. GQ

28. What is the significance of Roger Federer's presence in the "Big Three" alongside Rafael Nadal and Novak Djokovic for global tennis fandom?

a. Symbolizes unity in tennis

b. Drives intense competition

c. Attracts a diverse fan base

d. All of the above

29. In which year did Roger Federer become the first solo athlete to grace the cover of Vogue?

a. 2017

b. 2019

c. 2021

d. 2023

30. Which major global sporting event did Roger Federer withdraw from in 2016, disappointing fans and impacting his global popularity?

a. Olympic Games

b. FIFA World Cup

c. Ryder Cup

d. Super Bowl

ANSWERS

1. c

2. a

3. a

4. a

5. d

6. d

7. c

8. a

9. a

10. b

11. c

12. c

13. c

14. d

15. c

16. c

17. b

18. b

19. d

20. b

21. b

22. b

23. a

24. b

25. a

26. b

27. a

28. d

29. c

30. a

COACHING AND MENTORSHIP
QUESTION TIME!

1. Who was Roger Federer's primary coach during the early years of his professional tennis career?

a. Ivan Ljubicic

b. Stefan Edberg

c. Severin Luthi

d. Peter Lundgren

2. In 2016, Roger Federer added a new member to his coaching team. Who became his coach that year?

a. Paul Annacone

b. Tony Roche

c. Ivan Ljubicic

d. Stefan Edberg

3. Which former world No. 1 player served as a mentor to Roger Federer during his formative years on the ATP Tour?

a. Pete Sampras

b. Andre Agassi

c. Bjorn Borg

d. John McEnroe

4. In 2010, Roger Federer hired Paul Annacone as his coach. What significant achievement did Federer reach under Annacone's guidance?

a. Completed the Career Grand Slam

b. Surpassed 300 weeks as world No. 1

c. Won the Olympic gold medal

d. Won his 20th Grand Slam title

5. Which coach played a crucial role in Roger Federer's breakthrough year in 2003 when he won his first Grand Slam title?

a. Peter Lundgren

b. Ivan Ljubicic

c. Severin Luthi

d. Paul Annacone

6. In 2021, Roger Federer announced that he would be working with a new coach. Who was this coach?

a. Ivan Ljubicic

b. Stefan Edberg

c. Pierre Paganini

d. Christian Ruud

7. Who coached Roger Federer to his first Grand Slam title at Wimbledon in 2003?

　　a. Peter Lundgren

　　b. Paul Annacone

　　c. Tony Roche

　　d. Stefan Edberg

8. During Roger Federer's partnership with coach Peter Lundgren, which Grand Slam title did he win for the first time?

　　a. Australian Open

　　b. French Open

　　c. Wimbledon

　　d. US Open

9. Which coach has been a longtime collaborator with Roger Federer and played a key role in his training and fitness routines?

a. Ivan Ljubicic

b. Stefan Edberg

c. Pierre Paganini

d. Paul Annacone

10. In 2013, Roger Federer brought in a new coach to his team. Who was this coach?

a. Paul Annacone

b. Ivan Ljubicic

c. Stefan Edberg

d. Tony Roche

11. Which coach has been credited with helping Roger Federer make technical adjustments to his backhand, enhancing his overall game?

a. Ivan Ljubicic

b. Paul Annacone

c. Tony Roche

d. Stefan Edberg

12. Who served as Roger Federer's coach when he won the career Grand Slam by capturing the French Open title in 2009?

a. Peter Lundgren

b. Tony Roche

c. Severin Luthi

d. Paul Annacone

13. In 2014, Roger Federer appointed a new coach with whom he had a successful partnership, particularly at Wimbledon. Who was this coach?

a. Stefan Edberg

b. Ivan Ljubicic

c. Tony Roche

d. Paul Annacone

14. Which coach encouraged Roger Federer to adopt a more aggressive playing style, coming to the net more frequently?

a. Tony Roche

b. Ivan Ljubicic

c. Paul Annacone

d. Stefan Edberg

15. Roger Federer has often credited a former Grand Slam champion as his idol and someone whose playing style influenced him. Who is this player?

a. Rod Laver

b. Bjorn Borg

c. Pete Sampras

d. Andre Agassi

16. In 2020, Roger Federer underwent knee surgery and spent time recovering. During this period, who continued to support and mentor him in his fitness and rehabilitation?

a. Ivan Ljubicic

b. Pierre Paganini

c. Stefan Edberg

d. Tony Roche

17. Which coach played a significant role in Roger Federer's resurgence in 2017, where he won two Grand Slam titles?

a. Paul Annacone

b. Ivan Ljubicic

c. Stefan Edberg

d. Tony Roche

18. In 2015, Roger Federer hired a former world No. 3 player as his coach. Who was this coach?

a. Paul Annacone

b. Tony Roche

c. Ivan Ljubicic

d. Stefan Edberg

19. During his career, Roger Federer has worked with coaches from which country?

a. Sweden

b. Australia

c. Croatia

d. Switzerland

20. In 2017, Roger Federer hired a fitness trainer who played a crucial role in his physical conditioning. Who is this trainer?

a. Pierre Paganini

b. Stefan Edberg

c. Ivan Ljubicic

d. Tony Roche

21. Who was Roger Federer's coach during his historic 2017 Australian Open victory, where he defeated Rafael Nadal in the final?

a. Paul Annacone

b. Ivan Ljubicic

c. Stefan Edberg

d. Severin Luthi

22. In 2014, Roger Federer won his first Davis Cup title as a part of the Swiss team. Which coach supported him during the Davis Cup campaign?

a. Ivan Ljubicic

b. Stefan Edberg

c. Severin Luthi

d. Tony Roche

23. Roger Federer has often mentioned seeking advice and guidance from a fellow Swiss player during his career. Who is this player?

a. Stan Wawrinka

b. Marc Rosset

c. Martina Hingis

d. Timea Bacsinszky

24. During his partnership with coach Stefan Edberg, Roger Federer reached the Wimbledon final twice. In which years did he reach the final under Edberg's guidance?

a. 2013 and 2014

b. 2014 and 2015

c. 2015 and 2016

d. 2016 and 2017

25. Who has been Roger Federer's longest-serving coach, providing consistent guidance throughout various stages of his career?

a. Paul Annacone

b. Severin Luthi

c. Stefan Edberg

d. Tony Roche

26. In 2008, Roger Federer won the Olympic gold medal in doubles with his partner Stan Wawrinka. Who coached the Swiss team during the Olympics?

a. Ivan Ljubicic

b. Stefan Edberg

c. Tony Roche

d. Severin Luthi

27. Which coach has been associated with Roger Federer in the development of the "SABR" (Sneak Attack By Roger) tactic?

a. Stefan Edberg

b. Paul Annacone

c. Severin Luthi

d. Tony Roche

28. In 2020, Roger Federer announced that he had undergone another knee surgery. How did his long-time coach react to this news?

a. Expressed disappointment

b. Wished him a speedy recovery

c. Announced retirement as well

d. No public reaction was reported

29. Which coach has been instrumental in Roger Federer's training routines, emphasizing the importance of fitness in prolonging his career?

   a. Stefan Edberg

   b. Ivan Ljubicic

   c. Pierre Paganini

   d. Tony Roche

30. Roger Federer has often acknowledged the influence of a specific coach on his mental and emotional resilience. Who is this coach?

   a. Tony Roche

   b. Stefan Edberg

   c. Paul Annacone

   d. Severin Luthi

ANSWERS

1. Peter Lundgren

2. Ivan Ljubicic

3. Pete Sampras

4. Surpassed 300 weeks as world No. 1

5. Peter Lundgren

6. Pierre Paganini

7. Stefan Edberg

8. Wimbledon

9. Pierre Paganini

10. Stefan Edberg

11. Tony Roche

12. Severin Luthi

13. Stefan Edberg

14. Stefan Edberg

15. Pete Sampras

16. Pierre Paganini

17. Tony Roche

18. Ivan Ljubicic

19. Switzerland

20. Pierre Paganini

21. Ivan Ljubicic

22. Severin Luthi

23. Stan Wawrinka

24. 2014 and 2015

25. Severin Luthi

26. Severin Luthi

27. Stefan Edberg

28. Wished him a speedy recovery

29. Pierre Paganini

30. Severin Luthi

Printed in Great Britain
by Amazon

43547106R00086